SELF-MADE WOMAN

THE ULTIMATE GUIDE FOR SUCCESS-DRIVEN WOMEN IN THE WORKPLACE

Phoebe Bryant

For Dela.

CONTENTS

PREFACE

What does it mean to be self-made? The term is usually connected to a final state of achievement that one makes in their life; the suggestion being that they made it alone. Well, I believe self-made starts with a personal decision that is followed by smaller ones, and these decisions culminate into different stages of one's life where the risk is placed solely on the decision-maker. To be self-made is to hold exclusive responsibility for your decisions.

The decisions that I made about my career put me in the driver-seat and I knew that only I could be responsible for the outcomes. During my journey, I fell and I failed a lot. It was part of the experience. I sought help when I needed assistance, and I sought mentorship when I needed clarity. I guess, in this way, you could say that I didn't do it alone, but the decisions I made were mine. Right or wrong, I would live with the consequences. This is what self-made means to me.

As a single mother and head of my household, the duties of managing both my career and family were hard to balance, and my image was scrutinized more closely than that of my male counterparts. I work in a male-dominated field, where there's the traditional men's club. Despite my personal challenges with these politics, I chose to move forward, falling and failing, but always focused on my competencies, my achievements, and my goals.

I wrote this book, not to teach you to be political, but instead to give you a prototype of career success that can be applied in any company. This book is about recognizing the behaviors I once ignored that put me in career-limiting situations, and how you can avoid making the same mistakes.

You will find short stories throughout the book, which demonstrate situations that can occur in your day-to-day corporate experience. While these situations are drawn from real personal experiences, these stories and characters are fictional and are provided only as illustration. As you read each story, ask yourself if the circumstance is familiar to you: can you relate to the feelings and sentiments that these women have?

I hope that what follows will help you define yourself objectively and remain authentic while adapting to a workplace environment that may seem uncomfortable or foreign. I want you to be reassured that events and circumstances are constantly changing and that challenges that may seem unique to you are common, temporary, and don't have to always be faced alone. Generations of women before you have faced similar challenges and, like them, you can face them from a position of strength, authenticity and self-confidence.

CHAPTER ONE

INTRODUCTION

Have you ever found yourself frustrated at work because you:

- Don't understand the workplace dynamics?
- Get caught off guard by the politics at play?
- Can't seem to build the proper relationships?
- Struggle to communicate effectively with people inside and outside of your networking circle?

Workplace strategies are useful whether you are just starting out and unfamiliar with office politics, or are a seasoned professional in the workplace. If you are struggling to be taken seriously and are not being recognized for your abilities, there are strategies you can learn to help you manage your career more effectively. Working hard and being seen as the "work-horse" in the office is not the same as being seen as a leader and future CEO of a company. In this book, you will discover several strategies that cover fundamental areas of office life.

By not having the proper guidance and strategies to use at work, it's easy to become frustrated and angry by the everyday occurrences that push you away from your goals. Eventually, you'll realize that simply working harder isn't enough, and that it doesn't reduce the odds of you being in negative situations that can put you behind in your career.

The Myth

There is a myth about adaptation in the workplace that is believed by some women to their detriment. The myth is that if you adapt your behavior to that of successful men, you will stand out and be noticed for the same leadership qualities. Let me be clear: Mirroring the exact behaviors of your male coworkers will not be to your advantage. Either you run the risk of being seen as aggressive rather than assertive, or odious as opposed to agreeable. Women who work twice as hard to be the "better man" are not as effective as women who work smarter.

Adapting to the workplace requires balance. Every company has a culture that you will need to understand in order to navigate successfully within your day-to-day. This balance comes from staying authentic and being aware of the nuances that make up the company culture. Observe your environment: Do people generally come to meetings prepared, or is there time given at the start to get folks on the same page? Does management promote challenging the status-quo, or do you work in an environment that values its traditions and ways of working?

Working smart involves balancing your abilities and skills with the environment that you work in. For example, if you are an A-type personality that is always prepared and likes to have plans (and back-up plans for your plans), but work in an organization with flexible methods and unstructured work schedules, you will need to open up your schedule and allow for unscheduled tasks. It may be difficult to get used to, but anticipating impromptu events is how you balance the situation in your workplace.

What to Expect

This book is short and meant to be a quick read! There are seven chapters, each with stories that are built-in to illustrate specific learning objectives. The stories are examples of everyday work occurrences that can throw you off balance. They are designed to assist you in recognizing ineffective behaviors that you can correct so as to begin to operate above your current peak levels.

Part One: Chapters One – Three: These chapters focus on self-improvement and self-discipline. The pathway to any goal or achievement starts with how you think, feel, act and react. It is my belief that if you start with yourself, the rest is easier to accomplish. It was Henry Ford who said, "Whether you think you can, or you think you can't—you're right."

Part Two: Chapters Four – Five: The next two chapters focus on the influence you have on others around you. Being successful in anything you set out to achieve will usually involve other people performing some task to help you. The image you project and the relationships you build are important in this regard, as well as learning how to work with others you don't necessarily like.

Part Three: Chapters Six – Seven: The last section of the book covers the inevitability of workplace battles and how you can survive and navigate the battlefield. This was one of the hardest lessons for me to learn myself and I can't explain how lonely it feels when you're on the wrong side of the fight. There are strategies you can use to make sure you're well equipped, more knowledgeable, and less likely to make the same mistakes that I did.

Success is defined differently for women. For me, success was being able to thrive in an environment while navigating the politics and staying authentic. I wanted to build for myself the foundation from which I would model the rest of my career. I believe that with the right skills and strategies I can pursue whatever career path I want.

For others, success could mean financial freedom, or balancing work and family life. For women like me, being free from worry over financial matters and making quality time for the family is not only important, but essential. And while the strategies in this book focus on workplace dynamics, I believe they are the foundation from which you can achieve both of these goals.

This book wasn't written overnight, and neither was my career. I made it through my successes and failures to teach you the methods with the most value-add, and which I have found to be universally effective. I am self-made—now I am passing the baton on to you.

PART ONE

YOU

CHAPTER ONE

HOW

A woman walks into a shoe store. The store is crowded with shoppers and salespeople. They're busy, running around and helping their customers. The highest concentration of activity is centered around several racks of shoes on display. It appears those shoes are on clearance.

I'm never going to find what I'm looking for in this chaos, the woman thinks.

Alternatively, here's another way to frame it:

A woman walks into a shoe store. The store is crowded with shoppers and salespeople. They're busy, running around and helping their customers. The highest concentration of activity is centered around several racks of shoes on display. It appears those shoes are on clearance.

I can't believe I found this sale; I am going to get some good deals today! she thinks.

Work on your mind—frame, perceive, and think about life in a new and different way. When you take in a scene, your brain immediately uses attention filters to understand what it's seeing. Attention filters are like signposts or street signs that are easily recognizable to you. They are meant to alert you, or provide information. After attention filters are activated, the brain uses retrieval cues to retrieve relevant memories. A retrieval cue is a clue or prompt that is used to trigger the retrieval of your long-term memory.

In the first example, the woman may have had a bad shopping experience and what she remembered when presented with the situation was the chaos of it all: a busy atmosphere, lots of customers, and busy sales staff who only cared about selling her stuff she didn't need. Her recollection of her past experiences immediately influenced the way she framed the scene. Just like this woman, your thoughts are largely based on your experiences; whether shopping, driving, in the workplace or anywhere else, your experiences can dictate how you process the environment.

The first strategy you should know and practice in your professional life is the technique of framing—and it starts with your thoughts. Framing situations in a negative way can be disastrous to your career and your health. Simply put, negative framing invites frustrations, distractions and assumptions into your mind that can both bias you with negative perceptions and create the negative models your brain will store and use later. Negative framing means the glass is always half empty.

When you frame situations in a positive way, options become clearer and issues become less complex. Negative framing leads you to limited and pessimistic conclusions about the outcomes of the situation you are experiencing. Positive framing suggests more possibilities for positive outcomes now and in the future.

In this chapter, I discuss the importance of framing your thoughts so that you're not sidetracked by stressful ideas and misperceived circumstances.

The objectives covered are:

- Recognizing your thoughts, and
- Understanding how to frame

The following story illustrates what exactly it means to carry around a negative frame.

Welcome to Venicor

Storyline 1 – Chapter One

B randy Singh has just been promoted to her new position as a compliance analyst at Venicor Pharmaceutical, reporting to Jesse Barber, the senior compliance manager. Brandy has twelve years of experience in her field and she prides herself on being detail-oriented and a self-starter. She is thrilled about her new position because it allows her to branch out and work with people in different departments and at different levels in the organization. Her last boss was too high-strung, and it seemed that no matter how hard she tried, she could never satisfy him. So when this position opened up, she prayed hard for it.

Two weeks into her new job, Brandy is returning from a break when the admin, Donna Ryan, waves her down.

"Did you see Jesse?" Donna asks. "He was looking for you."

"No. Did he say what he wanted?"

"No. He said he'd catch you later."

Brandy goes back to her desk and checks her email and IM feed, but there is nothing from Jesse. She wonders what is so important that he'd come to her office. She shrugs and opens an analysis she had been working on for Jesse's boss, Linda Wilson, the head of the compliance department.

Just ten minutes later, Jesse pings her on IM.

knock, knock... He writes

hi she types back.

busy?

working on a thing for Linda but I can take a minute.

stop by? he writes.

sure she sends, and heads to Jesse's office.

Brandy is glad for the break. She isn't exactly sure what Linda wants in the report; maybe Jesse will have some advice.

Jesse greets Brandy warmly and waves her to a seat. He was one of the reasons she had looked forward to working at Venicor. He had been kind and supportive throughout the interview and training process and he had gone out of his way to make sure she was settling in okay.

"How are things going?" he asks.

"Good. I've worked on most of the regulations in my last job, so I think I've hit the ground running. And there's more windows over here which makes the office space brighter, so that's nice."

"It's not Google..."

"But what is?" Brandy says, and they laugh.

Jesse asks, "How are things with Linda?"

This sets off an alarm in Brandy's mind. She and Linda had met a few times, most recently about the report Brandy was working on. She had tried to get clarification from Linda about what the deliverable was, but she didn't think Linda had understood her questions and she had been reluctant to press.

"Fine," she ventures. "Why?"

"I just got the idea that maybe there was some friction there or something."

"Did Linda tell you that?"

"No, no, nothing like that," Jesse says, "but I heard a couple things, that's all. Anyway, don't worry about it. That's the way Linda is and everybody knows it."

"What way?"

"She runs hot and cold. She was totally for bringing you on, but now...you know. I should have given you the heads up. She's done this to people before."

"Yeah, I asked her for some clarification about what she wants this report to look like, but she wouldn't give me any help." Brandy was getting a bit nervous, but did her best not to show it.

"Yeah, that's Linda. Anyway, don't take it personally. Give it a couple weeks and she'll go after someone else." Jesse's words didn't paint a promising picture.

Back in her office, Brandy can't help but take it personally. To make matters even worse, Linda calls her to ask about the status of the report late that afternoon as Brandy is getting ready to leave.

Without any preamble, Linda blurts out, "So when can I expect that analysis?"

"Well, I was looking at the R&D procedures earlier and there's nothing about the new regulations in them."

"They're in the addendums. Didn't you get that during training?"

"Um, I don't know. I don't think so. Can you—"

"Really?" Linda cuts her off. "Well make sure you get that from Jesse. Or better yet, talk to Ted or Fred or whatever his name in IT; he'll send you the link to where we keep them on SharePoint."

"Okay, got it," Brandy says. "Ted in IT."

"So I can expect that by the end of the week, then?"

"End of the week, no problem. Thanks, Linda."

"Great. Don't stay too late, Brandy."

Brandy sighs and looks at the clock. It's 4:45 and it's her turn to make dinner, but she takes her coat off, texts her husband saying she is going to be late and then calls IT to find Ted or Fred somebody for the SharePoint link.

At the end of the week, Brandy presents her report to Linda and gets little from her but grunts and questions about why Brandy had done things the way she had. Brandy leaves the meeting with a feeling of doom and wonders if Linda is looking for reasons to get rid of her. She asks Jesse about it and he says, "No way. I probably would have heard something." That doesn't make Brandy feel any more confident about her future at Venicor.

~~~

Storyline One - Analysis

What was Brandy's initial frame of mind?

Brandy's original frame of mind about her new position was enthusiastic and hopeful. She was confident in herself and in her abilities. She viewed her new environment objectively and her demeanor was unassuming and cheerful. She had everything to look forward to.

Did Brandy's frame of mind change?

Yes. When Jesse told Brandy about Linda's disposition, she became suspicious. Brandy took Jesse's statements personally and went on to assume that Linda only saw the worst of her abilities even though, up to that point, she had not demonstrated any incompetence. Brandy's immediate conclusion about the impression she had given Linda was negative, even though the information she received from Jesse was hearsay and had no specific criticisms of her performance.

How did Brandy's frame of mind develop?

Brandy developed her frame of mind from a vague reference Jesse made about Linda's disposition with others. She had no signal from Linda directly to make her think that Linda felt she was incompetent. Most likely, Brandy framed the situation with Linda negatively because she was recalling a negative experience with her last boss. Prior job experiences, especially negative ones, can be your Achilles' heel when framing a new workplace environment.

What did Brandy do right or wrong?

Brandy's first instinct was to ask for clarification. That was right. She asked Jesse if Linda had mentioned anything specifically about her and Jesse said no. His clarification should have quashed her anxiety about Linda's opinion of her, but it didn't. Brandy brought her prior experience and the feeling of insecurity that came with it into her new workplace dynamic. That was wrong. At the end of this chapter, I'll discuss the warning signals that Brandy should have looked for; there is another way of framing that circumvents the tendency to draw conclusions based on incomplete information and past negative experiences, as explained in the next story.

The Meeting

Storyline Two – Chapter One

Jeanette Miles is a project manager at Venicor Pharmaceuticals working in the R&D department. She's only been with the company for two years, but she's been able to prove herself to be competent and results-driven in that time. She has recently been placed on a high-level project with broad responsibilities across several lines of businesses, and she still maintains some of the smaller projects that directly affect R&D.

Recently, her boss Andy Lortie held a meeting with his team announcing an organizational change. Andy would be working directly with a new business unit the company had just formed, and his team would now be reporting to Linda Collins.

After the meeting, Gary, one of Jeanette's coworkers, says, "I'm gonna go and dust off my resume."

"Why?" Jeanette asks.

"You've been here two years and you don't know about Linda?" Another colleague responds incredulously.

Jeanette shrugs. "I guess I don't."

"Are you a mind reader?" Gary asks, "'Cause if you're not, there's no way to please her. She wants something different every day."

"You've worked for her?"

"No," Gary says, "But I was friends with a guy that did. He's not here anymore. He said he couldn't take it anymore, but everybody knows Linda had him fired."

"Well, I guess I'll keep my eyes open, thanks."

Jeanette goes back to her office and gets back to work. She doesn't give much thought to what Gary or the other guy said, since it doesn't seem they have any direct experience with Linda. She knows that when things change, people are more than happy to put a negative spin on the outcome, but she doesn't see any point in worrying about the org change until she has concrete information to go off.

She would find out from Andy what Linda would likely need to know in terms of status about her projects. Then she'd pick his brain about Linda's work style, since she knew Andy had direct experience working with her. But until she knew Linda personally, Jeanette would reserve any judgment about her.

~~~

Storyline 2 - Analysis

What was Jeanette's frame of mind?

Jeanette's original frame about the org change was neutral; even though others around her had a negative reaction to the news they received, she was comfortable waiting until she had enough reliable information to draw her own conclusions.

Did Jeanette's frame of mind change?

No. Jeanette maintained the same neutral frame coming out of the meeting that she had going in.

How did Jeanette's frame of mind develop?

Jeanette used the information given in the meeting to deduce the answers to three questions:

1. What are the facts?

2. Has anything changed?

3. What, if anything, does the change mean to me?

Jeanette's framing strategy was systematic and deliberate. She took in the new information she was given in the meeting and applied a method of deduction that allowed her to stay objective.

What did Jeanette do right or wrong?

Jeanette sustained her positive frame of mind before, during and after the meeting. This was right. The method she used to deduce the information she received kept her from overthinking the scenario and making assumptions. Keeping her focus on factual information was the right approach to use. Even when confronted with colleagues spouting second-hand information and qualms about their new boss, Jeanette decided to reserve judgment.

Chapter One - Summary

The act of looking at, presenting, or thinking about something in a new or different way is called framing. One negative thought can lead to more negative thoughts and be counterproductive in the workplace. Making assumptions and overthinking are bad habits. Such an approach most commonly leads you to create a negative frame, which, most often, there is no rational premise for. In the workplace, negative thinking is always counterproductive to you and your coworkers because it takes the focus off your team's objectives.

You can combat the impulse of negative thinking by using the following positive framing strategy.

Positive Framing Strategy

1. Pause

Most people don't recognize negative thoughts as triggers; they just go with the feeling in the moment. This is the wrong approach. The most effective way to address negative triggers when they happen is to pause. Pausing is easy and effective because it allows you to do one important thing: take a quick assessment of how you're feeling. Taking just a few seconds to identify what the feeling is makes a huge difference in what comes next.

2. Recognize the Trigger

Recognize your thoughts and feelings as they're happening. When you do, you can reframe the negative ones immediately. The following thoughts and feelings are most common and can lead to making assumptions and overthinking:

- A sudden change in emotion, particularly to negative emotions (e.g., anxiety, frustration, anger)
- A negative thought or opinion about someone based on a past circumstance or imagined future event
- Feelings of insecurity
- Confusion

Triggers can be set off by any number of stimuli, such as an email, discussion, meeting, comment, memo, directive, or the simple expectation of any of these. The event preceding the trigger is good to know, but your reaction to it is more important.

3. Frame

Framing the feeling in your mind forces you to think and reason. When you begin to reason with how you feel, you steer your thoughts toward something different, which is the essence of framing. For example, if you've just been told that working hours have changed and you feel angry, you could turn your response to the situation around by first recognizing the trigger (your anger), pausing for a few seconds, and then reframing your feeling in a new way.

Instead of thinking "I feel angry," reframe it as, "I feel motivated." Your mind will reason with this new feeling even before you begin to feel it. While your mind is processing the new feeling you've framed, the old feeling immediately starts to dissipate, allowing you to form a new and more productive emotion.

In the second story, Jeanette not only reserves her judgment about Linda Collins after hearing negative criticisms, she also finds an advantage. While her colleagues are succumbing to their negative frames by reacting to them, Jeanette takes the time to go to a reliable source—her boss Andy—and learns information she can use to her advantage.

Strategy Takeaways

- ☐ Pause any time a negative thought enters your mind at work.

- ☐ Then, as soon as you can, write down the trigger, which is the feeling you had just before the thought entered your mind (e.g. anger, frustration, boredom, betrayal, etc.)

- ☐ Now frame it and replace the feeling you identified with a positive thought in your mind. Take your time and stay focused on the positive thought.

- ☐ Finally, write down the advantages you have by being at your job (e.g. the commute, training, experience).

Personal Notes

WHAT

What makes people want to control every aspect of their lives? According to Dr. Debra Reble, a licensed psychologist, "Control is a fear-based pattern stemming from a need for stability, security and predictability in our lives." This is especially true when faced with survival issues at work, because our jobs are tied to how we earn a living and how we construct our identities.

When feeling in control is successfully achieved, it creates a sense of security. Conversely, feeling a loss of control creates frustrations and fear that can lead to clouded judgment. It is important to understand that, in the workplace, all you have control over is your own thoughts, actions and reactions.

The external control factors that are prevalent in the workplace are tough to ignore. The employee/boss relationship has a control characteristic to it; the worker has a distinctive understanding that their boss is in control of their assignments, their performance assessment, and their pay increases.

In many organizations, managers or directors have the ability to promote careers or end them. So we act in ways that reduce the chances of us getting fired and try to increase the possibility of getting promoted. The challenge, however, is that the more we try to control these external factors at work, the more opportunities we have to be let down and feel out of control within ourselves.

For example, at work you will be challenged with many external factors like requests or demands from your boss, negative feedback from coworkers, and questions from newbies on the job, not to mention your daily tasks. It will not be possible to control absolutely everything, but it is possible to control how you respond to what happens. Controlling your response is an act of self-control; without it, you allow situations to control you.

How do you react to a rude email? Do you immediately respond negatively and then regret your emotional undertone after hitting "send?" If so, you've just allowed yourself to be controlled by an external event. It is called emotional reacting and it will never serve you well at work. In this chapter, I discuss self-control in the workplace and what you can do to understand it and practice it consistently.

The objectives I cover are:

- Defining self-control,
- Recognizing what you can control, and
- Applying strategies to stay focused on intended outcomes.

Self-control is an everyday challenge. In chapter one, Brandy had some challenges with her frame of mind. Let's see how well she does with her everyday challenges at Venicor.

Out With the Old, In With the New

Storyline Three - Chapter Two

Venicor Pharmaceutical has decided to expand its business and needs to be more cognizant of how it stores its records. To that end, it announces that it will be implementing a new records management system. Brandy Singh is on point as the subject matter expert in compliance, as policies will need to be reviewed and rewritten for the system, and Linda Collins is heading the initiative.

Brandy is excited about her new role. As subject matter expert, there is a lot to be done, and Jesse and Linda are both letting her run with an interesting project. She is wary of reporting directly to Linda for the project and wishes Jesse could give her more air cover, but so far things are going okay.

Her phone rings. It's Jesse. "Hey," he says. "How did it go in Quality?"

"Great," Brandy replies, "They're being really helpful. I've got their existing policies and procedures mapped, and they've got a lot of good ideas."

"No push-back on the new direction?"

"None at all. It sounds like they've been wanting this for a while."

"All I needed, thanks."

Just as she hangs up with Jesse, Brandy's computer chimes and she sees a new email from Linda. All it says is, "Status meeting Monday 10 a.m."

Brandy confirms her attendance and puts the meeting on her calendar.

***

At the meeting on Monday, Linda gets right to business: "Let's see the gap analysis report and go from there."

Brandy freezes for a moment and shuffles the papers she has with her. "It's not done yet," she says. "I do have the—"

"Brandy, we talked about that three weeks ago." Linda demands, "When am I going to see it?"

"We never—it's almost done, but you never put a date on it. I can get it to you by Wednesday, but I didn't think you needed it so soon."

"Then you should have asked," Linda quips. "I don't know how you start something like that without knowing when it's due. What have you been doing for the past three weeks?"

"Jesse has me working with Quality on procedure changes and on some other things. He needed that stuff done before we could move on to the next step."

Linda says, "I understand. I'll talk to Jesse about it."

***

Jesse calls Brandy into his office later that day.

"Linda's not happy. She says you've been sitting on that gap analysis. I don't need to tell you that you shouldn't be giving her reasons to wonder if you're the right person for this."

Brandy leans back in her seat and crossed her arms. "I can't believe you're putting this on me. Look, Linda never said when she needed the analysis, and she won't—or can't—tell me how she wants it to look. It's almost done, but I have no idea if it's what she wants. I mean, I've done most of it and I've also done everything you handed me."

She throws her arms up and continues "C'mon, Jesse, this is completely unfair! It's like I've got two bosses, and one of them can't be bothered to tell me what she wants. You know how she is."

Brandy feels herself tear up, and that makes her even angrier. She knows her face must be flushed bright red.

Jesse looks alarmed.

He holds his hands out and says, "Hey, it's okay, everything's going to work out. I'll try to get some direction on that gap report from Linda. You just work on that and I'll get you off the Quality thing so you'll be able to get it in on time."

"No!" Brandy loudly protests. She's crying now. "I've done a good job with Quality—"

"I'm not saying you haven't, but you're overwhelmed. Let's just dial that back and you can get Linda what she needs, okay?"

It isn't okay, Brandy thinks, but she doesn't know how to tell Jesse. She likes the projects she has been doing for him and she feels like she's been doing a good job on them. It isn't fair, she thinks. She is losing the important projects to spend time on the gap analysis that Linda will read once and forget about.

And never mind that she still doesn't know how to complete it in a way that will satisfy Linda.

~~~

Storyline Three - Analysis

What were the external factors in the story?

The story outlines three external factors. The first was the decision to implement a new records management system. The second was Linda's appointment as the program lead. The third was the tasks that Brandy was given.

Did Brandy control her response to the external factors?

No. Brandy did not control the external factors (the tasks given to her). The story ended in a painful, yet common, scenario in the workplace. It illustrates how Brandy got in her own way and ended up losing control of her emotions.

Brandy had the ability to take control and give herself an advantage. Brandy was apprehensive about clarifying the report details with Linda. She probably felt embarrassed or insecure about confirming the report once Linda had already explained it. But when she wasn't clear the first time, it was up to her to take control and get the clarity she needed.

We all know the saying, "There are no stupid questions," and we also know that most people don't believe that. It's normal to have feelings of apprehension when we need clarification on something that has already been discussed, and no one wants to be the one asking the stupid question.

But there is a strategy to phrasing questions differently. For example, when Linda described the report requirements to Brandy and Brandy was still unclear, she could have restated her limited grasp of the requirements and asked if she was correct in her understanding. If she had, the conversation between Brandy and

Linda might have gone quite differently:

Brandy: "So I'll keep the gap report focused on all the updated regulations and I'll have it to you by the end of the month."

Linda: "Actually, I'd like to see the focus on regulation 21 CFR and I'm going to need it in two weeks."

Chapter Two - Summary

Self-control is a skill like any other. Some people possess good communication skills, some possess good technical skills and others possess great creative skills. When we bump these skills up against each other, they all sound very specific. For example, we might say that Susan is a good communicator, but that she lacks technical skill. Some skills are specialized, which explains why some people can excel at a particular task involving that skill. Self-control, however, is a skill that everyone possesses, but most do not give themselves credit for it and don't exercise it as much as they could or should.

Self-Control Strategy

1. Master Your Internal Dialogue

Think about the kind of internal dialogue that you commonly entertain. You may identify phrases like: "He/she makes me so angry," or, "My job is stressing me out." These are dangerous statements that downplay your own personal power to recognize what you control. Affirmations are a good way to stay in control of your internal dialogue. There are plenty of positive affirmations that you can replay in your mind that will begin to change the automatic negative voice that keeps you distracted. Write down or collect a list of positive affirmations that you can repeat to yourself. Here are just a few:

- "I never sweat the small stuff."
- "I won't let anger control me; nothing at work is worth

getting angry about."

- "I trust myself to make the smartest and best decision for me."
- "I'd rather smile, it looks better on me."

2. Be Deliberate

Every person has self-control, but oftentimes this skill is repressed and underutilized. If you intend to be successful in the workplace, you must begin using this skill. For example, deciding to introduce yourself to someone in the elevator instead of following the status-quo of watching the floors pass or checking your phone. By stepping outside what you would normally do, you take yourself off automatic mode and into the realm of conscious choices. Be deliberate and do something different every day. A deliberate action on your part is practicing self-control. The best way to start being deliberate and doing something different is to recognize the things you do without thinking about, such as:

- Using the same cup/mug for coffee,
- Having the same thing for breakfast/lunch or dinner, or
- Playing the same radio station in the car on the way to work.

Start by deliberately doing something different with the smaller routines in your life first. Then work your way to deliberately changing the more significant things you do. Start small to build up your self-control discipline. As you get used to it, the automatic urges will be replaced by you thinking deliberately and taking deliberate action.

3. Control Your Focus

Always stay focused. This is an element of self-control that is harder to sustain. We live in a world that is full of distractions and instantaneous expectations that paying attention to one thing for too long feels like watching wet paint dry. The following workplace terms have diminished how we focus: mental switching, multitasking, and parallel planning. The idea of doing more than one thing at the same time is seen as an asset. The problem, however, is that our brains weren't developed to perform effectively in this way without sacrificing another controlling attribute to do so.

Staying focused requires clarifying what you can control and being focused only on those things. It should go without saying that the only thing you can control is yourself. However, workplace hierarchy can make it difficult to remember how much self-control you do have. So at work, keep focused on these control themes:

- "I am in control of my actions and reactions."
- "I am in control of how I manage information."
- "I am in control of what I focus on."

Strategy Takeaways

- ☐ Remove distracting thoughts by framing (*See Chapter One*).

- ☐ Recognize what you control (like the tasks assigned to you). If you're unclear about them, clarify the outcomes of the activities by *restating* your understanding of them to your boss.

- ☐ Remember what you control—you!

Personal Notes

CHAPTER THREE

WHY

How well do you know yourself? Not in terms of what you like and what you don't like, not in terms of what you can tolerate and what makes you uncomfortable, but in terms of the things that make you tick. Are you self-aware?

Self-awareness is having a clear view of your behaviors, feelings, thoughts and motivations, including your strengths and weaknesses. Self-awareness means that you understand how other people perceive you, your work style and your reactions to them in the moment. People who are self-aware work better with others, because they are always cognizant of what goes on around them and ready to adapt their work style to those they work with.

One of the benefits of self-awareness is the ability to interpret daily exchanges between yourself and others. Being able to do this well is an advantage in the workplace. The changes you make to the thoughts and perceptions in your mind—through framing— will allow you to adjust your emotions and responses to events.

Think about a time when you've regretted sending an emotionally-charged email, or regretted not speaking up in a meeting because you were focused on a comment that made you upset. Self-awareness is a key element of emotional intelligence and is an important factor in achieving success in the workplace.

Emotional Intelligence (EI) is the capacity to understand emotions and the effect they have on your thoughts. It is the ability to accurately perceive your emotions and adjust them to assist your thoughts and actions, promoting emotional and intellectual growth. In the workplace, emotional intelligence has two key benefits.

First, a person with high EI can understand what sets her off and she can harness those emotions and control them when need be. She can then use them to influence the achievement of a targeted outcome. Second, a woman able to read and react appropriately to the emotions of others is more effective at building relationships with coworkers, partners and customers.

Another benefit of EI is the ability to understand your work style. A person's working style is how she performs on the job and works with others. It's how she thinks or concentrates, and it is how she approaches her daily work and solves problems.

Everyone has a work style, or, said differently, a style they prefer, which they have learned or emulated and have adapted from others into their own. Self-aware people will generally be able to identify not only their own work style, but the work styles of others.

The objectives covered in this chapter are:

- Identifying your work style
- Recognizing coworker's work styles
- How to adapt to different work styles

Getting back to the work environment at Venicor, the following story will illustrate some work styles that may be familiar to you.

Linda Collins

Storyline Four - Chapter Three

The Records Management and Compliance System, or RMCS, project was in full swing. All hands were on deck for the effort. VP Jeff Drake had sent an organization-wide email announcing the project's kickoff and encouraged business units to cooperate with the project team members.

In her first meeting with Linda Collins, Jeanette provides Linda with a status of her projects and offers other transitional documentation for background.

Linda looks the documents over and says, "You did your homework. I don't mind telling you that I haven't gotten this kind of detail from anyone else."

"Thank you," Jeanette says. She doesn't care for the hint of criticism of other managers, but it isn't the kind of thing she comments on. She keeps herself focused on what Linda wants from her.

"RCMS is a big project; I know you know that." Linda continues, "If it doesn't go right, heads will roll. I want you to be on point from now on. I know you'll deliver, and I'm not so sure about some of the other team members."

Jeanette doesn't comment on that. "I can do whatever you need done," she says. "I need you to be as specific as you can about what you'd like to see: strategy, communication, team members, everything you think is important so we can hit 100% on this."

Linda nods and says, "Here's what I need from you," and they go over what she feels are the critical areas. Jeanette adds her own ideas and they put together an action plan.

At the RCMS project kick-off meeting two days later, Linda presents the project objectives, timeline and resource commitments.

"Jeff Drake is counting on me to see this through," she says, "and if there are issues about the timeline or objectives, now's the time to get them out in the open. Before we leave this room, we're all going to be on the same page; there won't be any room for missed deadlines or second thoughts after today, and everyone will be answerable to Jeff through me. I'm 100% committed to this project, and anyone who isn't is going to have to explain why if things don't go right."

One of the managers raises his hand and says, "I'm concerned about the resources we're committing to this. My department has projects that—"

"You'll just have to adjust your priorities," Linda cuts him off. "Anyone else?"

No one else has anything to add.

After the meeting, Jeanette passes two colleagues in the hall talking about Linda's presentation. One of them mocks her, saying, "Are there any questions? Good question. The answer is, 'You're fired.' Next?"

The second coworker laughs. "Yeah, that's Linda Collins 101."

Later in the day, Linda asks Jeanette to step into her office. She says, "It seems like everyone's on board. Just make sure you keep after them."

"So you feel the meeting went well?" Jeanette prods.

Linda nods. "I think they got the message. You shouldn't have any problems with them. Get me the minutes of the meeting. I'll have a look at them before I send them out."

"You'll have them by the end of the day," Jeanette replies.

"I know I can count on you," Linda says.

Jeanette wonders what Linda will see when she reads the minutes. Linda had solicited the opinions of the managers, then interrupted and cut them off at the knees. Jeanette knows she can shepherd the project to a successful conclusion, but she also understands that she'll have to manage up as much as she manages down to make it happen.

She knows that Linda is bound to create even more conflict than she already has. Jeanette is confident in the team's ability to see the project through, but even in its first days, she knows that Linda's communication style will be a significant hurdle.

~~~

Storyline Four - Analysis

Did Linda illustrate self-awareness?

No. Linda has no idea how she comes off to others. In her meeting with Jeanette, she criticized her direct reports and gave Jeanette the impression that if the project didn't go right, people on the team would be blamed, or worse, fired. Additionally, in the kick-off meeting she cut off a manager who was trying to raise a point that Linda had specifically asked for feedback on.

Did Jeanette illustrate self-awareness?

Yes. Jeanette was conscious of herself both in the meeting with Linda and in the kick-off meeting with the whole team. In the meeting with Linda, she didn't like the critique about her coworkers, but never let Linda see her discontent. In the kick-off, Jeanette allowed Linda to do the talking. Having recognized Linda's work style from her earlier meetings, she knew enough to know that Linda would want to take and keep the control in the meeting.

Furthermore, Jeanette was astute enough to determine if Linda knew how her work style affected others by asking Linda how she felt the meeting went. Linda's ignorance of the effect she had is also a useful nugget of information for Jeanette, and will directly affect how she manages both the other team members and Linda.

Chapter Three - Summary

Work styles influence the way we approach work and the people we work with. The differences between work styles can be seen in our differing opinions and ways of communicating, which can be the basis of conflict among coworkers. Being self-aware of your work style and how you are perceived by others in the workplace is an aspect of emotional intelligence (which you'll recall is the ability to build relationships among coworkers, partners and customers, and thereby influence targeted outcomes).

It is important to understand other people's work styles, but it's more important to start by understanding your own. The idea is that if you can recognize your own work style, you'll be more able to identify another person's work style, and you'll understand how to work with that person based on their style.

Adapting to work styles requires using three main skills: identifying, understanding and capitalizing. Earlier in the chapter, I stated that people who are self-aware will understand their own work style. But it's important to note that knowing how you like to work is not the same as understanding your work style. Understanding your own work style requires that you identify yourself with a work style.

Work Style Strategy

Use the IDEA framework to identify work styles. The four primary work styles are: Influencers, Directors, Empathizers, and Analyzers.

Influencers are generally optimistic in their thinking. They see lots of possibilities, they're very verbal, like to participate in groups, think intuitively (not step-by-step) and are creative—thinking outside of the box is one of their strengths.

Directors are concise and direct in their language, often using business-toned communication. They are independent, quick decision-makers, action-oriented and problem solvers. They are also very work or task-oriented.

Empathizers are the accommodators in the group; they like working with others and listen well to others' troubles. They are not very assertive about their own needs and like routine and predictability. Home life is very important to the empathizer and they often decorate their office space like a home away from home, with pictures and sentimental items on display.

Analyzers are systematic and thorough. They are concerned with accuracy and details, and are generally very careful and cautious. They often look at things critically and don't mind working alone.

It may be difficult to nail down the specific work style of an individual until you work with them. But as you do, strong attributes of that person will become noticeable and that should give you a sense of their work style.

Strategy Takeaways

- [ ] Recognize your personal work style.
- [ ] Using the same methods you used to recognize your work style, identify the work styles of your coworkers. To do this, get a sense of the attributes that they typically express. Remember, one person will not exhibit one work style

entirely; rather, most people are blends of at least two. Therefore, you have a 50/50 chance of sharing some work style attributes with your colleagues.

☐ Capitalize on your differences. For example, influencers who see possibilities will do well with a director who is a problem solver.

Personal Notes

PART TWO

———

YOUR
INFLUENCE

IMAGE IS EVERYTHING

In the movie *Working Girl,* the character Tess McGill takes advantage of a business opportunity while her boss is away on a ski trip. Tess is a struggling, yet ambitious secretary who does what she needs to close a deal that will boost her career. What is seen in the film is the transformation she goes through to craft an image that will allow her to promote her idea and also herself.

When you think about successful people in your organization, what image do they have in your mind? Professional image is the collection of personal assets and characteristics that signify perceptions of your capability and personality as judged by your boss, coworkers, partners, and customers. In the workplace, this means everything.

Image is important! It is your character, knowledge, work habits, self-confidence and associations. It's also developed from your family, neighborhood, values and beliefs. In society and in the workplace, people use their professional image to promote products and services. This chapter will discuss why and how you will use your professional image to promote yourself and make the right impressions.

In social psychology, the term "person perception" denotes how people use roles and social norms to form impressions of other people. This influences the conclusions we make about a person based upon our impressions. For example, a woman on a bus wearing hospital scrubs and sneakers with a pager on her hip and a cup of coffee in her hand will likely give the impression of a being doctor.

The reason this tendency to draw conclusions from limited information is so compelling is because it is most often right. People form impressions very quickly with little information and, because of this, it is important to understand what impressions you may be projecting in the workplace.

Physical appearance plays an important role in forming an impression. If you see a man come to work in a wrinkled shirt and pants, you may take him less seriously than you would a man who wears a clean and pressed suit and tie. Similarly, a woman who goes to work wearing a hot pink fuzzy sweater and a black miniskirt may be taken less seriously than a woman in a pantsuit. Perceptions are built from a person's beliefs and also by social categorization, or stereotyping.

Association and affiliation are also important perception factors in the workplace. The phrase "it's about who you know" is a good illustration of this. People who belong to a high-performing and popular work group are perceived as the group is perceived. A person is more likely to have a positive image if they are associated with the group or someone in the group. Likewise, negative perceptions can stick to a person affiliated with a group or person who has a negative image in the workplace.

Your skillset and the ability to do a job is part of your image too. Your image is a critical personal asset that can ruin or boost your chances of being successful in the workplace. There are people who spend just as much time and energy shaping their professional image as they do in getting the job done. The topics we discuss in this chapter explain why. Image should not be ignored or thought of as frivolous.

The objectives covered in this chapter are:

- Understanding your image,
- How to improve your image,
- The effects of a positive impression, and
- The effects of a negative impression.

So far, Jeanette has taken a careful approach in her work. Let's see how careful she is with her image.

The Sidekick

Storyline Five - Chapter Four

Jeanette Miles is off to a rocky start with her records management system implementation project at Venicor. Linda Collins' confrontational style at the kickoff meeting set the tone for the project. As a result, Jeanette has been finding it hard to gather the information she needs to finalize the project schedule.

Jeanette sits down with Joe, one of the managers on the project. She says, "I'm giving a status to Linda at the end of the week. What do you have for me?"

"Well, we're still working on freeing up some people from some other projects," Joe says. "We ought to know more by Friday."

"That's not going to work for me. You were at the meeting. Linda wants everyone on board on this."

"Yeah," Joe retorts, "we all know what Linda wants, but we can't just put everything else on hold. And you know that—can't you tell Linda the kind of problems this is causing? There's no way to talk to her."

"I'll talk to her about it, but I'm going to need that information by Friday," Jeanette says.

When Jeanette meets with Linda the next day, she tries to bring the issue to Linda's attention: "Some of the managers don't feel like their other projects are being respected. It sounds like committing what you want to records management is going to put them behind on other things."

Linda frowns and says, "It sounds to me like they need to

manage their resources and time better. Jeff Drake wants this done, so there's nothing to discuss. I'll light a fire under the people who are dragging their feet."

This isn't the conversation Jeanette is looking for, but she doesn't see a way to make Linda understand.

The next day, Joe catches her in the hall. "Thanks a lot!" he says. "Linda called me and read me the riot act this morning. I thought you were going to liaise with her instead of just being her mouthpiece."

Jeanette is taken aback. "That's what I'm doing, but management is set on the deadlines and the resource allocation. We're all just going to have to make do."

Joe snorts and says, "You know what your old group is calling you? The sidekick. Everyone's saying you've gone over to the dark side."

"I'm doing my job, Joe. What should I do, tell people what they want to hear and let them miss their deadlines?"

"I'm not telling you how to do your job. I'm just telling you what people are saying."

Later in her office, Jeanette thinks about how her colleagues' perception of her is going to make it difficult to manage them going forward. She's not sure what to do about it.

~~~

Storyline Five - Analysis

What was Jeanette's image?

Jeanette's lack of vigilance of her image has caused her coworkers to form a negative perspective of her. She is being perceived as her boss' pet or mouthpiece, and colleagues who once trusted her no longer do. Jeanette is ambitious and results-driven. She is also self-aware enough to realize that a negative image will not allow her to achieve her work objectives. Jeanette is in a complex position because she is working for a boss who has a negative image and her boss' negative image is sticking to her. The term "sidekick" suggests that the people-pleasing traits that once worked to her benefit are now being infected by her boss. She doubts it'll be easy to get people to follow her lead in the future if this nickname sticks around.

How will Jeanette need to work on her image?

Jeanette will need to start repairing her image immediately if she is to be successful with her project. As discussed earlier, people understand your image as a true representation of your character. Jeanette will need to start by addressing how people now see her.

Jeanette should:

1. *Laugh off the nickname*, but address the issue: she'll need to remind her colleagues that she has a sense of humor, but at the same time, lern exactly why the nickname is being used.

2. *Use opposing traits to highlight her own*: she'll need to watch her boss's mannerisms and be careful to do the opposite. If the boss doesn't smile much, she'll need to start smiling more; if the boss is commanding, she'll need to be more accommodating;

if the boss is always serious, she'll need to find more witty things to say that will break the ice and relieve the tension. This approach is similar to the "good cop, bad cop" tactic.

3. Get more face time: she'll need to get in front of team members not only for status reports, but also for discussing solutions to their challenges. She'll need to be seen as helping them, not as throwing them under the bus, even if she's done nothing to prompt such an outcome.

4. Manage her boss: Jeanette will need to manage her boss' expectations and illustrate a different way of doing things to get results. This could be a tricky area, so she'll need to be careful not to suggest that her boss' strategies are not working. The best way to position an idea to your boss is to make them think the idea was theirs to begin with.

If Jeanette follows these approaches, she'll quickly begin turning the tide of negative impressions about her into positive ones. There are some at Venicor, however, who manage their image a bit better, as illustrated in our next story.

Drake's Town Hall

Storyline Six - Chapter Four

Jeff Drake's star is on the rise at Venicor. As the VP of R&D, he's been with the company for only a year and is already well-respected. The new record compliance system is very popular with senior executives and the board of directors. It is expected to set a new standard for Venicor's commitment to excellence in its products.

Jeff carries himself with confidence at Venicor. He has a straight-shooter personality and has always been approachable. He likes to talk directly when communicating, which can often make his speech sound somewhat dictatorial, and he's usually inline with many of the other executives. Despite his boldness, however, he has unique delivery in his communication—people often respond to his humor, and he is usually the butt of his own jokes. Today, Jeff is hosting a town hall meeting to answer questions about R&D's new initiatives and direction.

"I've heard through the rumor mill that when people see me coming, they say 'run and hide' because I'm always coming up with new things for you to do," he mentions during his speech. This gets a laugh. "Fittingly, last holiday's gift exchange I was given a new name plate: the seeker." Another laugh.

Then he says, "But I don't want you to worry. Questions?"

Susan, one of the managers, raises her hand. "Where do you see the new initiatives in terms of priorities? Some of the deadlines and resource commitments are going to be a little tough to meet."

Jeff nods and says, "We all have a lot on our plate right now.

We're making an effort to reduce loads in the target areas. I don't want anyone pulling their hair out to make this happen."

He points to his mostly-bald head and says, "I want to keep what little I've got, so let's keep the hair-pulling to a minimum." This gets another laugh.

"You all know your own teams and projects best. If you have any issues, kick them upstairs and we'll get them sorted out. "

Most of the employees approve of this approach, though some are wondering at the similarities in tone between Jeff and Linda. Still, Jeff seems professional and approachable, and the meeting attendees leave feeling better about R&D's new direction.

~~~

Storyline Six - Analysis

What was Jeff's image?

Jeff's image is demanding, but open. He positions himself well in front of an audience because he takes the time to solicit questions and understand their concerns. Jeff's character is stern, but not intimidating. He gets along well with most of the other executives and he knows when to joke and when to provide support.

How will Jeff need to work on his image?

Jeff will not need to do much in terms of changing his image, but he will need to maintain it. Image, just like any other work technique, needs to be managed. Jeff will need to make sure he is consistent with the image he portrays, because the minute he alters it (putting people off or declining invitations from workers beneath his position, for example), he runs the risk of gaining a new image that is less attractive, like being seen as fickle, or worse, disingenuous.

A great example of a good image gone bad because of shifting ideals and tone can be seen in the US presidential race of 2012'. Presidential candidate Mitt Romney was caught on camera commenting to a small group of people that he intended to focus on a predetermined percentage of the American population. 47% of the population, he said, were not going to vote for him because they were dependent on the government.

The remarks were inconsistent with the image he was portraying to his constituents in general. When the video surfaced, it changed his image so dramatically that it still sticks to him today.

Jeff will need to ensure that he manages his good image, because with it and his ability to do his job, he will go far.

Chapter Four - Summary

Whether you're looking for a promotion or wanting to get noticed, consider improving your image around the workplace. In the 1988 movie *Working Girl*, the character Tess McGill saw an opportunity to promote her business idea. She knew right away that, in order to be taken seriously, she had to work on her image. Having the right image allowed her to project the authority necessary to get the deal done.

When companies want to promote their products and services, they use positive images and promotional material, and sometimes use celebrity endorsements to promote their products. Having a positive image and associating with people who carry positive images is an asset that should be used, cultivated and managed.

Image influences the perceptions people have of you. A negative image will create a negative impression and, similarly, a positive image will create an agreeable impression. People commonly use first impressions to draw conclusions about people they know very little about. In the workplace, this can work either to your advantage or against you.

There are three areas in which your image should be developed and managed: self-image, environment-image, and associate-image. These three areas are important to know because changes to any of the three may affect the others.

There's a good example of this in an episode of a popular sitcom called Seinfeld. The character Jerry had just started dating an attractive lady. Everything from her hair to the way she dresses is very agreeable. She carries herself in a way that he likes and he feels lucky to have met a lady like her to date. His enthusiasm compels him to brag about her to his friends.

One day, he visits her at her apartment. As he walks in, he notices that it's a complete mess. Her clothes are tossed about everywhere. It looks like her clothes are thrown everywhere—on the floor, the couch and on top of the coffee table. To make matters worse, the attractive lady's apartment has a bad smell. Jerry's impression of this woman immediately changes and he stops dating her.

The episode was meant to be funny and everything about the circumstance is exaggerated, but it illustrates that first impressions can sometimes be misleading and that second impressions can be just as important as the first. The first impression Jerry had of the woman was a "person perception." The woman was attractive in her appearance and dress. It stemmed from how the woman carried herself, or her self-image. The positive impression, however, didn't extend to the rest of her image.

Next, Jerry saw the woman's home (her environment image), and it didn't fit the person perception he originally had of her. The two conflicting images, self and environment, created a negative impression of the woman's overall image. Image maintenance requires the commitment to create a consistent image over time and across the various areas of perception.

Think about the same woman in the workplace. If the initial impression she creates in an interview is different from the impression she creates while at work, she may face challenges or even lose her job eventually because the original impression she gave was not an accurate representation of who she really is. When you focus on your image at work, it should cover all three areas: self, environment, and other people's perceptions of you. An example of developing your image with other people was captured in the "Drake's Town Hall" story. Creating a good impression for others includes the way you approach, speak to, listen to and treat the people you work with and work for.

Image Strategy

1. Organize Your Wardrobe!

Take an assessment of your closet. Your closet should be neat enough that you can scan over your wardrobe quickly. Keep your work clothes separate from the clothes you don't wear to work. When you separate the clothes you don't wear to work from the ones you do, you're less inclined to try to get away with wearing something too distracting or inappropriate to work. Consolidate your work clothes so you can see them better. Start with suits, suit separates, then blouses

Remove clothes that don't fit to another area in your closet. I do this myself, and keep clothes that are too small in my closet as goal pieces. I will try them on periodically to assess how much weight I've lost. It's ok to use this method of motivation, just keep those pieces to the side and not mixed in with the work clothes that do fit. Next, take note of key pieces that you need to replace or that are missing. Then create a shopping list and always maintain your work wardrobe. Remember, classic looks never go out of style.

2. Keep Up Your Appearance

Appearance at work simply means how you carry yourself. It includes your wardrobe, but also takes into account your hair, make-up, and general hygiene. You can have a great wardrobe, but if your general appearance is untidy, the wardrobe won't be noticed. Keep simple hairstyles for work if you don't have the time to maintain a trendier look. Make-up is important to most women and I know it is for me too. However, keep your make-up modest and unassuming. General hygiene is important too. If you like to work out at lunch, remember that a quick shower afterwards should be seriously considered (more like never avoided).

Your appearance does extend beyond clothes, hair, make-up and hygiene. You should consider everything around you, as it all contributes to your overall image. For example, your workspace is part of your image too. Be sure to keep your workspace tidy and neat.

Strategy Takeaways

Self-image - Wardrobe Do's:

- ☐ Keep your wardrobe appropriate and unassuming. Use neutrals and solids in navy, brown, gray, red, and black.

- ☐ Your wardrobe doesn't have to be boring; nice prints can be worn with a blouse or scarf.

- ☐ Wear clothes that fit you well and are comfortable.

- ☐ Keep your work wardrobe separate from the clothes you'd wear out with girlfriends.

- ☐ Skirts should be an appropriate length; if you're not sure what this means, then use 3 inches above the knee as your guide.

- ☐ Keep your heels at an appropriate height—four inches is a recommended max.

☐ Keep your clothes clean and pressed at all times; the wrinkled or crinkled look is never workplace-appropriate.

☐ Keep an outfit in your office (if you can) for the occasions where you spill food on your top or skirt, or when your period comes unexpectedly.

Self-image - Wardrobe Don'ts:

☐ Wear loud and distracting clothes or colors; don't mimic trendy looks.

☐ Wear clothes that don't fit you well.

☐ Wear flip-flops to work (not even on casual Friday).

☐ Dress outside the culture: if the workplace environment is corporate casual, don't go to work like you're going to the club or going to work on Wall Street.

Self-image - Personal Hygiene Do's

☐ Shower in the morning, if you can.

☐ Keep your skin well-moisturized.

☐ Keep a deodorant spray or stick in your desk or purse, just in case.

☐ Keep your teeth white; consider whitening if you drink lots of coffee.

☐ Keep your breath fresh (use breath mints after lunch).

☐ Keep your nails cut and manicured or use acrylics and gels, filed and polished.

Self-image - Personal Hygiene Don'ts:

- ☐ Keep chipped nail polish on your nails.
- ☐ Go to work with wet hair!
- ☐ Wear face jewelry (if you have face piercings, use the smallest studs; stay away from hoops—they are too distracting).

Self-image - Speech Do's:

- ☐ Speak clearly and pleasantly.
- ☐ Use an appropriate tone (inside voice).
- ☐ Always use positive words when you can.
- ☐ Self-image - Speech Don'ts:
- ☐ Yell or speak loudly.
- ☐ Grunt or use other non-speech sounds as a form of communication.

Self-image - Body language Do's:

- ☐ Smile (people don't do this enough!)
- ☐ Always sit and stand straight.
- ☐ Look people in the eyes when speaking to them.
- ☐ Give firm handshakes.

Self-image - Environment Image Do's:

- ☐ Keep your car tidy; if it's a mess, don't volunteer to be a driver on a lunch outing.
- ☐ Keep your desk appropriately "busy," but not too messy.
- ☐ If you have an office, keep it appropriately furnished. Keep

personal items to a minimum.

Self-image - Environment Don'ts:

☐ Keep a moldy coffee mug or cup(s) on your desk.

☐ Keep inappropriate items on your desk, for example, Tarot cards, pillows from home, figurines or gaming devices.

Self-image - How You Treat Other People Do's:

☐ Listen to people.

☐ Never appear too busy to help, even if you are.

☐ Be thrifty with your words; use them well.

☐ Use humor to break the ice.

Self-image - How You Treat Other People Don'ts:

☐ Interrupt a person when they're speaking.

☐ Smirk or have a smug expression on your face.

☐ Gossip (always tempting but never a good idea).

☐ Get in the habit of giving speeches; make your point, then move on.

Personal Notes

CHAPTER FIVE

RELATIONSHIPS MATTER

Effective communication in business is important to good "working" relationships. The people we see every day at work, or even occasionally during the course of the day, are relationship candidates. They are team members, colleagues, bosses, ex-bosses, administrators, the IT guy (or gal!), the folks in facilities, even the office cleaning personnel.

Relationships add value to your overall personal growth and to the growth of your career. Irrespective of your job or industry, relationships permeate your work. Look at it this way: without people, there is no organization, but an individual. And even an organization of one requires having good relationships with others—its customers.

George Levinger, psychologist and author of several publications on relationships, developed the five-stage relationship model. The five stages—attraction, building, continuing, deterioration and ending—represent the phases people pass through during the life cycle of a relationship. Levinger indicates that the five stages are related to any relationship, regardless of whether it is with a significant other, friend, or family member. I discuss them here because they are a good illustration of how working relationships can develop, and being familiar with them will give you an idea of the process.

The first stage is the attraction stage. The attraction stage can also be associated with first impressions. You may be attracted to another's dress, appearance, professional posture in a face-to-face meeting, or by the praise or interest they show in you. An example of this stage in practice could be the first time you meet a new coworker:

You've been told by a colleague that the new marketing director is "sharp," someone they've known from prior employment and "have always worked well with." With this bias in mind, subsequently, you meet this person with the same expectation and are pleased to find that there was nothing to contradict the commendation.

The second stage is the *building* stage. Here, two people will share mutual interests, aspects of personality, attitudes or anything with which to start a conversation in the hopes of building a foundation. However, the building stage can also end before it even begins because of an inability to find common ground. An example of this stage in practice is seen when an innocent hello at the water cooler goes bad when an unsolicited opinion by one colleague about a political candidate is not shared by the other. An otherwise amenable relationship is stunted by a simple comment, and the perception created in the one offended leaves him or her with no desire to build the relationship further.

The third stage, the *continuation* (or endurance) stage, happens after coworkers pass the building stage and have determined the relationship is worth pursuing. Both put forth an effort to enhance the positive factors of the relationship by making an effort to speak to each other throughout the day or meet for lunch occasionally.

An example of this would be demonstrations of friendliness and trust. During this phase, mutual trust and respect is present. Each person is learning more about each other, respecting boundaries, and always willing to help.

The fourth stage is *deterioration*, or what I like to call the "ambiguity stage." This is when one or both parties are no longer in the continuation stage, but are not quite ready to call it quits. Working relationships that fall into this category can bounce from ambiguity back to continuation, depending on the circumstances. The ambiguity part in this stage means that one or both parties are pursuing different relationships in areas that no longer share common goals or objectives. A once-active, socializing friendship will turn into an occasional hello at the water cooler during this stage.

The fifth and last stage is the ending stage. The ending stage is when the ambiguity stage does not bounce back to the continuation stage and lingers until a passive response by one or either parties, or even an active response, fails to reignite the working relationship. An example of this stage in practice could be empty-interest comments to hang out after work, or a missed lunch meeting that ends with a failure to reschedule.

The best place to invest in and maintain a healthy working relationship is in the building stage. This is the most neutral stage of the working relationship model. Although you may have many colleagues that fall into the continuing stage, keep it simple and limit these relationships to a few.

Work friends in the continuing stage should be the exception and not the rule. The reason being that situations can become awkward or uncomfortable if your work friend begins to involve you in workplace drama. Establishing boundaries with your work friends is important and will only help to advance your career.

The objectives covered in this chapter are:

- Identifying the relationship stage
- Identifying the relationship stage transition
- How to prevent going into the deterioration and ending stage

Getting back to Brandy, let's see how well she does forming relationships at Venicor.

Brandy

Storyline Seven - Chapter Five

B randy finally managed to score kudos with Linda for her report analysis. After reflecting on how she could have handled herself better with her boss Jesse, she becomes laser-focused on finishing the report and getting back on track with her career. She also realizes that the relationships she has at work are as important as the work she does there.

Ted, another compliance analyst, has the office next to hers. He is married and has two sets of twins, which he talks about often. He has pictures of his family on his desk. Brandy is in Ted's office to go over the timeline for their current project and she uses it as an opportunity to build a relationship with Ted.

She points to a picture of his family and says, "These are your twins? My sister has twins too."

"That's them," Ted smiles.

"I can't figure out why people get twins confused," Brandy remarks. "I can always tell my nephews apart."

"I know," Ted says. "It bugs me when people just throw their hands up like it's impossible to know which is which. I think they're as much different as they are similar."

They talk a little longer about it and when Brandy leaves, she feels that she and Ted have made a connection.

On her way out, Brandy runs into Cindy, a business operations manager who works on the same floor, but in a different department. Cindy is carrying a plate with some of her famous pastries and offers Brandy one.

"This is so great," Brandy says. "I skipped breakfast and I thought I was going to have to get another dry bagel at the café."

Cindy encourages, "Take two. But leave the plain chocolate— Linda loves those."

"You must know her pretty well if you know what kind of pastries she likes."

"Oh yeah, Linda and I worked together before we came to Venicor."

"Really?" Brandy asks. "How was that?"

"I loved working with Linda. She was always really supportive and she's so funny."

"That's awesome," Brandy says. "Are you going to try to get a transfer to her department?"

"That's the plan. She told me as soon as a spot opens up, I'm in."

Brandy takes her pastries and heads back to her office, thinking that she can improve her relationship with Linda by trying to notice her sense of humor and the supportiveness that Cindy has experienced.

Later that week, Brandy meets with Jesse and Rick, a senior analyst. Rick is newly married and very ambitious, and Brandy respects his abilities, but she can't seem to get on the right foot with him. She has tried to be friendly to him, but he always seems too busy to talk to her.

In the meeting, Rick behaves condescendingly, asking her, "Do you know that Title 21 section 390 supersedes the definition of commerce?"

Brandy responds, "Yes, I'm familiar."

Later, Rick does it again: "You know that Title 21 covers processing, right?"

Again, Brandy responds politely and confidently that she's aware of this, but she can't help but feel that Rick thinks she's incompetent or inexperienced. She knows that a good working relationship with him will help her, but she can't figure out a way to make him see that she's a peer and not just "the help."

Storyline Seven - Analysis

What relationship stage is Brandy in with her colleagues?

We see very clearly in the story that Brandy is in the building stage. Brady has a new fire in her belly that didn't exist before. She is determined to firm her position in the company and knows that it starts with meeting the people who are in her immediate line of sight. It doesn't take much to find commonalities with the people you work with if you're looking for them. So many people don't take the time to begin this stage, but it starts with you.

How will Brandy transition from the building stage to the continuing or endurance stage?

Moving between relationship stages should happen organically with a degree of control. That is to say, it takes two people to successfully transition in a relationship and the intention to do so must come from both sides. However, you should understand why the relationship is transitioning. The building stage is the best place to remain in workplace relationships. Taking a workplace relationship to the next level should be done in a controlled and deliberate way.

For example, let's say Brandy and Cindy begin to find they have a lot in common both professionally and personally. Their working relationship goes from casual discussions to weekly lunch dates. Then they go to drinks after work and, finally, to meeting outside work for social events. The friendship could blossom and they could be better coworkers for it.

Now let's say Linda places Cindy in her organization, then changes the department and puts Brandy under Cindy's leadership instead of Jesse's. The friendship could end up becoming complicated and uncomfortable for both women. Brandy would do well to keep the relationships she builds in the "building" stage unless there is a compelling reason for a change.

How can Brandy build a relationship with Rick, who doesn't seem to respect her?

The relationship dynamic between Brandy and Rick is an interesting one. Rick has demonstrated, either innocently or purposefully, that he doesn't fully recognize Brandy's capabilities. It would not serve Brandy to immediately see Rick's behavior as facetious. The very notion can throw her off her objective. If Rick is being facetious then he would have accomplished his objective.

Instead, Brandy should continue to keep Rick in the building phase. If Rick's intentions are to discredit Brandy, she will know soon enough, as Rick is ambitious and he'll continue his line of questioning even after she's demonstrated her ability. Recognizing Rick's intentions should be on Brandy's radar until she has confirmed his animosity toward her. Brandy should continue to make innocent small talk and try to find something she and Rick have in common.

Chapter Five - Summary

Levinger's five-stage relationship model depicts the path all relationships will travel during their lifetime. While his theory wasn't specifically aimed toward working relationships, it still has strong relevance to how people connect in the office. The workplace is a dynamic and changing environment. It takes communication and cooperation to run a business and, without the proper establishment of relationships, it can be difficult or even impossible to get things done.

Among the five stages (attracting, building, continuing, deteriorating and ending), the building stage is the area in which you should focus on keeping the majority of your work relationships. The building stage explores mutual interests and aspects of personality—the commonalities with which to start a conversation in hopes of building a foundation. This stage does not go beyond small common interests and can be sustained by regular intervals of genuine engagement.

The continuing and deterioration stages—the middle stages— are more volatile stages of a relationship. Unlike personal relationships, work relationships are more fluid because of the workplace environment. A work relationship can move very quickly through the stages and it may not be clear why a relationship has gone from building straight to deterioration.

Relationship Strategy

1. Keep Your Relationships Positive

There is not one sure strategy to prevent a work relationship from going into the deterioration or ambiguity stage. The main reason is that it takes two: one person can't genuinely control a work relationship. However, keep yourself from falling victim to negative talk and you can avoid becoming the subject of work gossip and sustain a good image in the office.

2. Don't Underestimate Your Relationship Circles

Strong work relationships improve your ability to gain support for ideas and solutions you'll want to champion. They're also a mitigation approach for barriers that will challenge you along the way. An example of this is receiving helpful information before anyone else does. Depending on who you know, you can find out almost anything in the workplace, even the things you shouldn't know. Things like who's getting fired or hired, and whose budgets haven't been approved.

You can also learn valuable information, like the relationship differences among stakeholders you need to influence. For example, let's say you have a solution you want to push forward and you learn that Tim in marketing doesn't have the respect of Dan in sales. So you decide to seed your idea to Susan in marketing instead, because she and Dan have a better relationship. Utilizing work relationships like this separates those who succeed in the workplace and those who don't.

Strategy Takeaways

☐ Communicate with respect in every interaction.

☐ Recognize good work and give praise; call people out for doing a good job.

☐ Follow through and follow up on all of your actions.

☐ Listen more than you talk; don't rush in to give advice.

☐ Work out concerns with the source, not with others.

☐ Say "Thank you!" when others provide assistance or support.

☐ Focus on issues when you discuss work matters and problems.

☐ Put yourself in the other person's shoes.

☐ Be direct and sincere as a normal practice.

☐ Encourage feedback.

Personal Notes

PART THREE

YOUR CONFLICTS

SEPARATE FROM THE NEGATIVE

There are events and circumstances that will occur over the course of your career that will leave you feeling like you've just come out of a battle. There are people you will come across who will single you out and deliberately try to make you look bad—and the sad part of this is that it really happens. Part of the dynamics in the workplace includes heavy politicking. You will face subtle hostilities and passive aggressive behaviors that will get under your skin. Bad behavior is inexcusable, but reacting to it distracts from the objectives that are important to your career success.

Rudeness at work is not unusual and studies find that it's on the rise. 98% of workers polled in a study led by Christine Porath of Georgetown University's McDonough School of Business and Christine Pearson of Thunderbird School of Global Management, have reported experiencing uncivil behavior. In 2011, half said they were treated rudely at least once a week. This means that almost everyone in the workplace has experienced or witnessed rude or uncivil behavior.

Moreover, what one considers rude and uncivil, another considers a passionate opinion or strong personality. Opportunities to feel ill-used are rife, and there's not much that can be done about it unless rude behavior rises to the level of harassment. What *can* be done is controlling how you react (see Chapter Two). This will help your career and allow you to feel in control, rather than like a victim.

As women, we tend to be in tune with our emotions. This allows us to identify incivility and rude undertones more easily. Then again, we also could be more susceptible to taking offense to these undertones and strong personalities.

A comment or uncivil gesture could be frustrating to witness or endure. It could easily become the unexpected factor that keeps you from raising an important issue or idea. And while rude comments are inexcusable, it is important to recognize when the behavior is distracting you from achieving a business objective.

In addition to stress and attrition, incivility produces certain effects in and reactions from the people who are its targets. The same study from Porath and Pearson shows that 48% of the people decrease their work effort, 38% decrease the quality of their work and 78% lose their original commitment to the company. Many who are in extremely rude environments eventually quit, but those environments are the exception.

Most of us are in the middle, where incivilities are not everyday occurrences, and are nowhere near the level of harassment. This middle ground is a place where rude behavior is subtle and passive aggression is common. When quitting is not an option, the answer starts with understanding how to react and still get results.

Professionalism dictates that people possess thoughtfulness and consideration, and that they have a healthy attitude about work. Professionals have a strong work ethic. They can adapt and be fluid in a changing environment.

For a professional, these qualities are neither negotiable nor flexible. The journey of professionalism, therefore, requires the right tools and strategies to support the sustainment of professional conduct. Part of the sustainment effort includes being prepared for and knowing how to react to uncivil gestures, rude people and subtle hostilities.

Reactions can be instinctual. Think about the instinctual reaction you have when you put your hand in a flame: you immediately withdraw your hand for fear of being burned. While that kind of reaction is automatic, learned behaviors can also, of course, become automatic reactions to the right triggers.

If you have a temper, you might react to impoliteness with anger. That anger is a learned response and, unlike pulling your hand away from a fire, it can be unlearned. Recognizing the various kinds of incivility, recognizing your automatic responses and learning how best to react are important career skills.

The objectives covered in this chapter are:

- Recognizing passive aggression and subtle hostilities
- Understanding what it means to react negatively
- Learning how to react to bad behaviors and still get results

Even at Venicor there are uncivil behaviors, as you'll read next.

Loose Words Need Thick Skin

Storyline Eight - Chapter Six

In a way, the office environment at Venicor mimics a playground: some children play nice and some don't. Donna Ryan has three more years before she is eligible to retire. She's been working in the field of administration since before computers were commonplace in the office environment.

During the course of her career, she has held important positions supporting vice presidents and heads of corporations, men who were very demanding straight-shooters. A recent acquisition of her former employer brought her to Venicor. Since her tenure at Venicor, she's gotten on well. She supports the corporate business risk and applications group headed by Linda Collins and has been under Linda's direct leadership for nine months.

One day, Linda stops by Donna's desk to enquire about the capital request she's been working on. Donna usually facilitates the signatures required for requests over $250,000, and there are generally no delays. Linda asks, "What's the status of the signatures?"

"Andy Walberg hasn't gotten back yet," Donna says.

Linda is clearly upset. She leans forward and demands, "When were you going to let me know about that? If Andy's holding this project up, don't you think that's something I need to know?"

"I'll get back to him today and get you an answer on that," Donna calmly responds.

"Don't bother. I'll handle it." Linda storms off.

The whole scene has been witnessed by Jen Marchione from business ops, Rick Pazinni, a senior compliance analyst, and one of Rick's direct reports, Michael.

Jen says, "Jeez, is she always like that?"

"That's just Linda's way. She doesn't mean anything by it," Donna replies.

"I don't know how you put up with it," Jen says. "If my boss talked to me like that, I wouldn't even come into work."

"You can't take it personally," Rick adds. "Linda's got bigger balls than most of the guys around here."

"No shit," Michael swears.

Rick smiles and says, "At least she looks better in pants than most of the men in the office."

"Too much information," Michael laughs. "I'm outta here."

They walk away, laughing and joking about Linda.

Jen is uncomfortable and doesn't know what else to say to Donna. So she says goodbye and walks away too.

***

Back in her office, Linda calls Andy Walberg. He's always been friendly to her, but he's a peer and she knows she doesn't have any way to make him deliver the signature. When he answers, she says, "Andy? Linda. My admin told me you haven't gotten that request back to her."

"Hi, Linda! How have you been?"

"I'm good. Do you have any information about that request?"

Linda presses.

"You know," Andy says, "I've been meaning to tell you what a great job you're doing on the records project. Everybody says it's going well."

Linda is impatient with Andy's compliments. She says, "Thanks, that's really nice of you. If there's any problem with the request, you know...if you have any questions, I can address them now while I have you on the phone."

"Oh, no, there's no problem. It all looks good."

"So when do you think I can expect that signature?"

"It's the first thing on my list as soon as I finish what I'm on now."

"So I can expect that today?" Linda asks?

"Sure. Today or tomorrow. Soon as I finish what's on my desk."

"Great. I'll look for it later today then."

"Good talking to you, Linda. Keep up the good work."

"Thanks, Andy. Talk soon."

After she hangs up, Linda is bothered that she wasn't able to get a firm commitment from Andy, but she doesn't know what to do about it. He's put her in a corner. If she demands the signature, or even a date for delivery, she risks coming off as unreasonable.

Several days pass and Andy still hasn't gotten the request back to her. She becomes even shorter in her interactions with Donna. Donna understands that it's Linda's frustration with Andy that is driving her rude behavior. She doesn't care for it, but she doesn't bring it up with Linda either.

~~~

Storyline Eight - Analysis

Is Donna's reaction to Linda appropriate?

Yes. Donna has an obliging attitude to Linda's communication style. While Linda's style of communication is not ideal, it's also not prohibited. Linda's mistake in the exchange with Donna is that she isn't aware that her tactless behavior is noticed by others in the office, and that it's negatively affecting her image. Donna's reaction was appropriate in that she didn't react to Linda in a way that would exacerbate Linda's frustrations further.

Donna's had experience with communication styles similar to Linda's over the years and has learned that staying focused affords her the patience to continue to do her job. Donna stayed professional and responded with willingness to take immediate action. It didn't make Donna look weak by keeping her composure. It made her look strong. Uncivil behavior is bad for an office environment, but it takes two opposing forces to cause friction and it's far better to stay neutral when tempers flare.

Was Rick's criticism of Linda appropriate?

No. Rick's criticism of Linda was not appropriate. His comments were an example of sexual harassment; it is prohibited in the workplace and taken seriously by every company worth working for. Sexual harassment's legal definition is unwelcome sexual advances, requests for sexual favors, and other verbal or physical conduct of a sexual nature that tends to create a hostile or offensive work environment.

Comments like Rick's often go unchecked and, over time, can

become a real problem. At the very least, his comments were also a form of subtle hostility toward Linda and women in general. It would have been appropriate for Donna and Jen (and Michael, for that matter) to report the remarks to HR.

When comments that border both sexual harassment and subtle hostility are part of a conversation, they should be called out and addressed. However, if the comment elicits a negative emotion, the wrong reaction could make matters worse. One bad comment should never be overshadowed by another.

In the story, Jen felt uncomfortable after hearing Rick's comment and did not know what to say, so she walked away. Donna also witnessed the comment and said nothing in the moment. While this reaction is not ideal, a negative response could have diluted the real offense.

What was the passive aggressive example in the story?

Andy clearly showed in his behavior that he was not comfortable signing off on the capital request. Passive aggression is often not immediately evident, but the signs, however subtle, are enough to notice. Andy never directly committed a date to Linda even though she clearly asked for one more than once. In addition, Andy's amiable demeanor on the phone was in direct contrast to his actions afterward.

Passive aggression is prevalent in the workplace. It often goes unnoticed and masks the conflict that exists. You should be cognizant of the subtleties that exist in passive-aggressive behavior.

Chapter Six - Summary

The workplace is the new adult playground. Conference areas and boardrooms have replaced swing sets and slides, but the dynamics are similar, and not all children play well together. Like a playground, cliques will form and the children group with friends with similar interests. Adults, like children, will have disagreements, and on occasion you will get bullied. As a professional, you have to assimilate yourself to the playground as best you can, and that involves your reaction to uncivil behaviors as they arise.

Like on the playground, teasing and bullying do occur in the office. When it happens, you have to know yourself well enough to know what you can tolerate. Teasing and bullying have no place in a professional environment and the stress it can have on you is not worth absorbing for long periods of time. If you find that you're in an environment that fosters an environment for bad behavior, find another job, and then resign.

Incivility once in a while, however, is not worth leaving a job over. Moreover, the difference between a strong personality and offensive behavior, or banter and crude speech is often a matter of perspective. If you complain every time someone raises their voice, you risk being perceived as rigid and too hard to work with. No one will want to work with you if they feel like they'll be walking on eggshells when you're around.

The following strategy should be practiced to develop the habit of recognizing when you've felt offended and defuse your emotions long enough to think rationally. Remember, taking things personally can be counterproductive. When you can control your reactions to offensive events in the workplace, you give yourself the power to achieve more.

No-Offense Strategy

1. Remember To Pause

Pausing is easy and effective because it allows you to do a very important thing: it gives you the ability to take a quick assessment of what you're feeling. When you take just an instant to consciously consider what you're feeling, it makes a huge difference in how you react.

By pausing to decide if you're feeling anger, frustration, dejection, or apprehension in a particular moment, you allow yourself to take control of the only variable that is entirely yours. The simple act of stopping to recognize what you're experiencing is like making sure both hands are on the wheel—you are ready to steer the situation.

Pausing may seem passive, but think about it: you have just identified an emotion that usually elicits an immediate response. Pausing allows you to identify what you're feeling and prevents you from reacting from an emotional place. The goal is to decouple what's happening on the emotional level from your response. You do nothing (initially) because this allows you to think through the scenario, understand it, and respond in a more reasoned and measured way.

2. Clarify What You Heard

It's amazing what people sometimes say in a work environment and not all comments are appropriate. Comments that sound sexist or racist in nature are not tolerated in the workplace and should be addressed immediately. Use the clarifying technique: repeat back to the offender what you heard.

The purpose is twofold. By repeating what you heard, you refrain from making a response you may regret, like shouting back a similar insult, which may put you at risk as well. The other purpose of clarifying is to illustrate how the comment sounded to you. It doesn't matter if the person intended it to sound differently—if it came off as sexist or racist to you, it's inappropriate.

3. Take Appropriate Action

In the instance of a sexist or racist comment, report the incident in writing immediately to your supervisor/boss by sending an email, and copy HR. It is everyone's responsibility to ensure that inappropriate sexist or racist behavior is not tolerated. In the instance of a rude comment that was clearly aimed at you, maintain your professionalism. Nobody likes a jerk and they always look bad, especially when their comments backfire and don't elicit a similar response.

A great example of this technique being used was when South Carolina Representative Joe Wilson yelled out, "You Lie!" to the President during the State of the Union speech in 2009. Joe Wilson yelled out while the President was outlining mandates of the healthcare coverage for undocumented immigrants. Clearly caught off guard, the first thing President Obama did was pause. Then, after a brief moment he calmly said, "not true," and continued with his speech.

If you break down this strategy, you will clearly see how the President used each element of it. The pause came first (this may also be instinctive for some people because normally you don't expect someone to be rude). Then, instead of reacting, the President did nothing initially, instead waving his index finger in the direction of the representative, as if giving a silent reprimand. The situation did not warrant clarification, since he was giving a speech, so the President maintained his professionalism, remained calm and said, "not true." The action he took was to acknowledge the truth in his statement and move on.

Remember, it was Mark Twain who said, "Never argue with a fool. Onlookers may not be able to tell the difference." The action items below will remind you what to do when you encounter a confrontation or offensive remark in the workplace.

Strategy Takeaways

☐ Emulate the type of behavior you expect others to give you.

☐ Practice pausing when someone has just insulted you or has acted inappropriately.

☐ If someone insults you, instead of reacting, clarify what you heard.

☐ Finally, take action and remain professional.

Personal Notes

CHOOSE YOUR BATTLES

---

n *The Art of War*, Sun Tzu writes, "Focus on the object of war and proper engagement." Fighting just to fight is a sure way to lose. First, decide what—if anything—there is to be won, and then choose the strategy most likely to achieve that outcome. It's quite natural for battles to pop up in the workplace. Everyone has their own goals, many of which may be quite different from company and group goals; work can become a battleground of egos and politicking, where agendas have priority over accountability and image takes precedence over competence. Battles can start with the simplest provocation and businesses objectives are lost when personal sides become the focus. Battles should never be fought for the purposes of posturing or for retribution if they are to be fought at all.

The workplace should not be a battlefield, even if some prefer to treat it as such. Nonetheless, battles do occur. Conflicts, which can turn spiteful, can create an atmosphere of distraction. They become matters of prolonged gossip, loose talk and unnecessary entertainment. When a person's mindset, emotional intelligence and self-control are weak, confrontations over even small issues are common.

You will not always be able to stop a battle from happening in the workplace and you cannot avoid them all. The best you can do is to choose a smart engagement strategy. Said differently, choosing your battles starts with identifying the conflict and knowing which engagement strategy to use.

The first thing to note about workplace battles is the environment. The workplace is neutral territory. The biggest misconception people have when waging war against a colleague is that their environment is a personal extension of themselves or of the other person. This is the reason why some people become so passionate about change. Understanding this can assist you in identifying the causes of conflict and why you may be directly or indirectly connected to it.

Once you understand the cause of conflict, the next step is analyzing the conflict by separating facts from opinion. For example, what would you do if the head of the sales division wages war with the head of the IT division over the disbursement strategy of new iPads for the organization? You are on the project team responsible for shipping iPads to the different divisions and now you get calls from the executives in sales wanting their new iPads before the folks in marketing get theirs. You are now in a battle you didn't start.

First, start with the facts. In this scenario, the project has already received leadership direction; you also know from experience that the sales executives have significant influence in the organization. People in the organization who "take care" of the folks in sales are always rewarded. The fact in this scenario is that *an approved logistical plan is being challenged.* The opinions are: (1) the urgent need for iPads for the sales folks, and (2) your own idea of being rewarded for "taking care" of the sales team.

Now that the facts are separated from the opinions, it is easier to choose the right engagement approach. Using the objective as the area of focus, which is *the distribution of new iPads*, you should determine if modifying the logistical plan will *strengthen* or weaken the objective. Of course, there would be a lot to consider, especially the downstream effects of altering the plan without careful study.

As long as the objective remains the focus, you have better odds of coming out of the battle with little or no harm done to your career. In the above scenario, it is not important that I tell you what should be done. Remember, the principle is called "choose your battles." What is important is the approach you take in making the right decision for yourself.

There will be times in your career when you will need to stand for something, which may initiate a battle. If you choose to fight, understand that you should never fight a battle you cannot win. Everyone will need to make this decision at least once in their career, and while battles are common, none are worth getting fired over. It may be that there are issues that lead you to decide to seek employment elsewhere, but that decision should serve your career and purposes. There are strategies you'll want to use to help you decide whether to engage or not.

First, decide if the odds are in your favor and know who you're going to battle with. Know who you're dealing with and do not offend the wrong person. For example, a person working in the mailroom may not want to go toe-to-toe with a senior executive in business development. In this case, you will need an ally, someone at that same level as the executive, a proxy that has more experience and connections.

Next, do some research and gain support by planting small seeds for your initiative. Socialize discreetly and stay away from details until you've gained commitment. You never want to say too much too soon, as it may be used against you later. Find common ground and mutual interests first.

Finally, stay focused on the objective. Do not let your emotions or opinions get in the way of the objective. Align your objectives to those of the company; this will help to validate your claim and attract allies. People need to feel that they are backing something common to that of the company's core goals. Most people don't want to get dragged into a personal fight, and backing company goals gives them cover if things blow up.

The objectives covered in this chapter are:

- Understanding work conflicts
- How to sort fact from opinion
- Knowing when to fight or stay neutral

You've read about Brandy, Jeanette and Linda's different circumstances and how they've handled them. By now you shouldn't be surprised that they have battles brewing at Venicor. How will these ladies fair in the final story?

The Last Battle

Storyline 9 - Chapter Seven

The new compliance system has just hit its peak at Venicor. All hands are on deck and tensions are running high. Brandy is busier than ever as the subject matter expert on the project, and while she's been developing good relationships, she and Rick still haven't hit it off.

Rick stops by her office with some questions about the project. "You took care of that regulatory thing, right?" he asks.

Brandy has learned not to react to his near-constant checking up on her. She says, "Three days ago. If you need the details, I'm sure Jesse will share the report with you."

"You know, I was thinking that with all that you've got going on, if you need me to help out with some of the more complex legal stuff, I'd be happy to pitch in."

Now Brandy understands why Rick stopped by: he doesn't want to be left out of the project, and he's hoping to poach some of her credit. There's no way she's going to let that happen, but she doesn't see any point in worsening their relationship.

"That's great of you to offer," she says. "Why don't I go over what I've got and get back to you in the next couple of days?"

At lunch with Ted, Rick is angry. He says, "She doesn't even know what she's doing half the time. She totally blew me off. Man, if I were doing her project, she'd be getting me coffee, 'cause no way would I let her touch anything important."

Ted smirks and says, "Yeah, well don't tell her that; she might start crying."

"What do you mean?"

"Yeah, this thing happened before you got hired on. She was having some kind of discussion with Jesse—not an argument or anything, you know?—and she totally freaked out, started sobbing and yelling at him and everything. Nan told me you could hear the whole thing even though Jesse's door was shut."

***

Back in the office, Jeanette also has her hands full as the PM on the project. She's managed to work past her nickname and has been strategically setting herself apart from Linda. On the other hand, she's had a harder time getting Linda to see her own follies. Her attempts to steer Linda away from offending people and toward using a different approach have only stoked the flames higher, causing Linda to become even more aggressive.

Over coffee, Jeanette's friend Marc asks, "What's going on with Linda? She threw you under the bus at the meeting."

"Everyone's under a lot of stress these days," she says.

Marc laughs. "That's classic Jeanette: put a good spin on everything. I get it, you don't want to gossip. I just wanted to make sure you're watching your back."

Jeanette smiles and says, "Back, front, top, bottom: I got it covered."

But to herself, she admits she's not sure. She wants to go to Jeff Drake about it. She hadn't worried much about succeeding on the project before, but now that it's clear Linda is actively working against her, she's not so confident. The project is career-critical for her, and if it goes wrong, the promotion she's aiming for will be in jeopardy.

She looks back at Marc and says, "Actually, it's not going as smoothly as I wanted, but it's not like I can go over Linda's head. If someone else were to go to Jeff Drake, that'd be one thing, but no way can I do it."

"Someone might do that," Marc smiles.

Jeanette smiles back knowingly and says, "Yeah, someone might."

Meanwhile, Linda is stressed about the project. She feels she's not getting the support she needs to be successful. There's always something or someone holding up progress at every turn and she feels that Jeanette is not carrying her weight in mitigating the risks. She's gone from overseeing the effort to micromanaging tasks she deems critical. Linda had thought that Jeanette was the right person to handle the small stuff, but she's just not tough enough and she often takes sides against her.

At a meeting that week, Linda presents her status. She closes her laptop and turns to the next person at the table, expecting his presentation next. But Andy interrupts. He says, "Are you sure that's the best approach?"

Linda is taken aback and doesn't know what to say immediately. "What do you mean?"

Andy speaks slowly now, coming just short of the tone used with deaf/foreign/stupid people in sitcoms. "Do you think that's the best approach?"

"Well, obviously," Linda snaps. "If there were a better strategy,

I'd be using that, wouldn't I? What specifically do you want to know? I'd have thought if you had any questions, you would have brought them up weeks ago."

Andy puts his hands up in an "I surrender" gesture, and everyone at the table but Linda understands that suddenly she's being painted as someone that can't be reasoned with.

"I didn't have any questions before, but now I'm not sure. Specifically," he parrots her use of the word as a set up for the punchline, "I can't understand the capital request you sent to me. Why are we using the lines of business for requirements building and testing? In the past, we've always gone to contractors for that kind of thing, and honestly, as stretched thin as we are, I don't know why you're not going off the reservation this time."

Linda scowls. "I looked at contractors, but we can do it better in-house."

"It doesn't look that way. I hate to say it, but I'm hearing that this is the bottleneck." Andy turns to the man on his left. "Lee?"

Lee looks very uncomfortable, but he says, "I don't know if I'd call it a bottleneck, but there have been some resourcing issues on my end. Far as I know, everyone's doing their best—"

"Exactly," Andy interjects. "If we're doing the best we can do and it's still not happening, I think we need to bring somebody in." Lee opens his mouth to finish his sentence, but Linda interrupts him.

"Look, Andy, if there's a problem here, maybe you should look in your own backyard. When I sent that request to you—"

Jeff Drake breaks in. "Okay, people, let's not get sidetracked.

We'll finish up with the statuses and then I'll make a decision about contractors. Agreed?" He looks around the table and gets nods from everyone. Andy smiles.

Later that day, Marc stops by Jeff Drake's office. He looks a bit uneasy, and Jeff invites him to sit. "What's on your mind, Marc?"

Marc is instantly put at ease that Jeff remembers him. He says, "I'm not one to jump the chain of command, but there's something I wanted to say that's been bugging me."

Jeff holds up a hand and smiles. "I'm gonna let you off the hook here. You've worked pretty closely with Jeanette, right?" Marc nods. Jeff says, "It's about the meeting the other day, am I right? Jeanette got roughed up a little."

Marc is relieved. "That's it exactly. I don't have anything against Linda, but—"

"I understand. I appreciate you coming in."

Marc thanks him and leaves.

Jeff calls Jesse and asks, "How are things going in your world?"

"Some bumps, some bruises, the usual," Jesse responds. "Anything in particular you need to know?"

"I'm just putting out some feelers. How is Linda doing on this thing?"

"She's...well, she's Linda. She's smart, she's quick and...and she's always the first person in the office and the last one out."

"But there are some issues." Jeff prods. "Some bumps and bruises, right?"

"Something like that," Jesse admits.

They speak for a little while longer and then Jeff has a similar conversation with Donna.

Two days later, Jeanette checks in with Linda and finds her fuming. Linda nearly shouts: "Jeff Drake's bringing in some consultants!"

Jeanette knows to play this carefully. She says, "Well, there's a lot riding on this. As far as I'm concerned, more manpower is a vote of confidence, and we can use the help."

Linda points her finger at Jeanette and says, "That attitude is the problem. The only thing I asked of everybody is total commitment to the project, and this is what I get. If we don't circle the wagons, we're going to lose control of the project."

Jeanette ignores the accusation and says, "I don't know what to tell you. If Jeff Drake wants to bring people in, that's the way it's going to be. It seems to me that the best thing we can do now is play nice with the consultants. We do that, we finish the project, everybody wins."

Linda is too angry to continue the conversation and tells Jeanette she has calls to make.

***

Two weeks later, based on the assessment of the consultants, an outside firm is hired to complete the initiative. Linda has been unable to work well with the consultants and is removed from the project. Jeanette, who has done everything she could to help them, is tapped as the in-house liaison to the outside firm.

Jeanette runs into Brandy in the hall not long after and says, "Walk with me for a minute, will you?"

They don't know each other well, but Brandy has always felt Jeanette is professional and respectful of her efforts. "Sure," she agrees.

"I heard about that situation with Rick. You good?" Jeanette asks.

Brandy surprises herself by laughing. "Oh, yeah, I'm fine. He's been trying to push me, you know? But I don't give him anything to work with," she smiles.

"Word is he was yelling at you."

"It's no big deal. What I really think is he couldn't get a reaction out of me and got frustrated and kind of blew his cool. It's not a thing, but thanks for checking on me."

"Good to hear it. Another thing: you used to work with the Quo Vadis guys, right?"

"The contractors? Yeah, a few years ago. If you've got any concerns about them, don't—they're pros, and they'll get it done."

"What I'm looking for is someone to second-chair me on liaising with them, and I think you're it."

"Really? That sounds great," Brandy says.

~~~

Storyline 9 - Analysis

What are the conflicts at play?

The first conflict is between Brandy and Rick. Brandy has done what she could to build a healthy work relationship with Rick, but like any relationship, it takes two to tango and Rick clearly isn't interested. The conflict that exists between Brandy and Rick is subtle. Rick has personal ambitions and sees Brandy as a threat. He's repeatedly questioned Brandy on basic job knowledge, hoping to throw her off her game and demonstrate that he's the better choice for the best projects.

The second conflict is with Linda and Jeanette. This conflict is trickier, as it involves an employee/boss relationship. Jeanette feels that her credibility among her coworkers has been put in jeopardy because of Linda's work style. Linda feels that the project is stalling due to not everyone working as hard as she is. Jeanette is her right hand and Linda feels Jeanette's been too soft in managing the team, and since Linda attributes job/work failures to self-failure, she blames Jeanette as the PM for all project issues.

The third conflict is between Andy and Linda. Andy sees Linda as a bully and generally doesn't like her, though he would never admit his bias. Because of this, instead of sharing strategy feedback with Linda, he holds back and blindsides her publicly, relishing the feeling of retribution—giving her a taste of her own medicine. Linda doesn't get Andy and has never bothered to try and build a relationship with him. She sees him like she sees everyone: as a tool. Because he isn't giving her what she wants on this project, she views him as a bottleneck in her success and a thorn in her side.

The last conflict is with Jeff and Linda. This conflict is very subtle, but it exists. While Linda is very calculating, thorough and clear, she's also seen as abrasive and not a team player. Jeff, being the leader in the organization, needs a team that can play well together. He sees Linda as the prima donna star player that hogs the ball instead of passing in an effort to gain all the recognition.

It bothers Jeff to see an unbalanced team and Linda's name is always at the center of team-dynamic issues. The project is Jeff's baby; he is the executive sponsor and its success or failure will have a lot of visibility and a consequent effect on his career. He is willing to sacrifice a star player for the advancement of the team.

Linda on the other hand doesn't know there's a conflict with Jeff; she's blind to it, as she's blind to everyone. This is the most dangerous kind of conflict to be involved in. As the old saying goes, "Keep your friends close, and your enemies closer." That's good advice, but if you don't know who your enemies are, it doesn't do you any good.

What are the facts versus opinions in each conflict?

Brandy v. Rick:

Fact - Brandy is on the project team for the compliance project.

Opinion(s) - Rick thinks he can do a better job than Brandy.

Jeanette v. Linda:

Fact - The project is having issues.

Opinion(s) - Jeanette thinks Linda is a threat to the project and her goal of getting a promotion, and Linda thinks Jeanette is not carrying her weight and is being too soft.

Andy v. Linda:

Fact - Linda needs Andy's signature on a requisition.

Opinion(s) - Andy doesn't care for Linda's work style, and Linda thinks Andy is a bottleneck to the project.

Jeff v. Linda:

Fact - Linda is leading the compliance project.

Opinion(s) - Jeff doesn't care for Linda's work style; he thinks she's bringing down the team.

When analyzing a conflict, try to pull out the primary fact. Then put yourself in your opponent's shoes and restate the fact. If the fact can be disputed, then it's not a fact. For example, in the Jeff v. Linda conflict, one might deduce that Linda is not well liked and use it as a fact. However, Linda's perspective would undoubtedly be different and, therefore, it is disqualified as a fact. But Linda is the lead for the compliance project, and that cannot be disputed by either side.

Opinions are easier to identify. Use just one to summarize each person's opinion. This may seem difficult as there may be lots of opinions and each of them may seem relevant. It's prudent to remember there are usually only two sides to a conflict.

Who chose to battle in each conflict?

In the first conflict, Rick chose the battle. He is set on trying to discredit Brandy and it's become his personal agenda to do so. In the second conflict, Jeanette chose not to battle Linda directly. Instead, she chose to use a proxy to go over her head by speaking with Jeff.

In the third conflict, Linda chose to fight with Andy over his concerns with the project. In the last conflict, Jeff chose the battle, albeit covertly. It's almost unfair to call the last conflict a true conflict, especially since Linda is unaware that the conflict exists. But conflicts aren't fair and blind conflicts happen all the time in the workplace.

Chapter Seven - Summary

Personal goals differ from company goals and the workplace can become a battleground of people lobbying for their personal agendas. Battles can start with or without provocation and a focus on the business' objectives is often lost when personal agendas become the focus. Conflicts cannot be avoided and, sometimes, trying to avoid a conflict only prolongs it. Choosing an engagement strategy is the best way to choose and win your battles.

Battle Strategy

1. Identify the Cause of the Conflict

Choosing a battle strategy starts with identifying the cause of the conflict and understanding why you are directly or indirectly connected to it.

2. Separate Facts from Opinion

You must then separate fact from opinion to analyze the conflict. The reason for this is that knowing the difference between fact and opinion allows you to choose a smart engagement approach. For example, Rick mistook opinion (Brandy is easily upset) for fact, and his strategy (to discredit her by making her upset publically) failed.

Finally, you should consider the objective of the battle and decide if moving in a certain direction will weaken or strengthen your chances of achieving the objective. For example, Linda's objective (to retain control of the project and advance her career) was not served by her reluctance to cooperate with the consultants.

3. Know When to Go to Battle

So how do you know when to go to battle or stay neutral? In most cases, it is best to stay neutral in any battle. If you find yourself in the middle of someone else's battle, use your engagement strategy to understand the conflict and weigh the objective. Again, you may not always have a choice of whether or not to participate. In that case, the choice you make is how to engage (as Lee did in the meeting with Linda and Andy). You always have the choice of how to engage.

Strategy Takeaways

- ☐ Understand the conflict and identify the conflict type (e.g. different work style, boss/employee, communication breakdown, etc.)

- ☐ Understand how and why you're directly or indirectly involved.

- ☐ Separate fact from opinion.

- ☐ Identify the objective and stay focused on it.

- ☐ Decide if the objective is strengthened or weakened by the battle; if weakened by the battle, stay away from it.

- ☐ If the objective is strengthened by the battle, find support for your initiative.

- ☐ Seed your initiative discreetly.

- ☐ Know your opponent; do not under-estimate them.

- ☐ Never fight a battle you can't win.

Epilogue

Through the book, we've followed three professional women. Each of them had something to learn, and they all were challenged with having to choose their battles. The following summaries cover each woman's finale at Venicor:

Brandy wins her battle with Rick by developing better relationships with the firm that took over the project. In a twist, the firm happens to be a company she used to work for and with whom she still has strong relationship ties with.

Jeanette saw the writing on the wall when the firm came in to assess the project. She deduced from her meeting with Jeff Drake that Linda was on her way out the door and began to seek opportunities outside Venicor. Once the dust settled and news came down that Linda was off the project, Jeanette surprised Linda by giving her notice of her resignation. She landed a new gig with the firm that came in to do the assessment and left Venicor with a good impression of her professionalism by recruiting Brandy to take over her responsibilities.

Finally, Linda decided to seek out an executive coach. After being pulled away from the compliance project, she was able to reflect on it more objectively. She knew that there were areas in which she needed better mentoring and made a commitment to herself to work on them. Linda found a coach, and Venicor found a new senior director.

Personal Notes

CONCLUSION

The stories in the book were developed to give you a clear and relatable view of how we sometimes get in our own way. In today's work environment, it is not enough to possess technical skills, because technical skills will not benefit you when politics are at play. How we frame our outside world, personal lives and relationships affects how we act and react to situations at work.

In order to succeed in the workplace, we women must not only demonstrate our technical prowess, but also our disciplined emotional strength. If leading a large company or building a strong business is what you desire, you must first lead yourself—build yourself. You cannot expect to control your career unless you learn to control yourself first.

The workplace is first and foremost a social environment. Of course, in any organization, you'll learn what the company's objectives are, receive memos, and attend team meetings to understand what your team goals are. However, the most important duty you have to yourself is to understand the company's culture. In order to do that, you need to understand your coworkers and understand yourself.

Self-awareness is often described as a form of emotional intelligence and it has received a lot of attention in the last decade for being an important factor of success. In the workplace, everyone has their unique work style, as do you, and being able to understand and recognize the different types of workstyles will give you more agility as you navigate through your day.

The first three strategies discussed in this book (framing, self-control and self-awareness) are methods you can use to build a strong foundation while you build your brand at work. The perception others have of you is bound in the image you portray. Equally as important to remember is that your image can be your halo, or it can be your downfall. Don't get caught up into thinking that you don't have an image, or that image is about materialism. It is not—far from it. You have an image even if you don't know what it is. If you don't know what it is and if you are not controlling your image, you are allowing others to control it for you—that is a dangerous position to take in the workplace.

Whether you have a role that puts you in an office, school or university environment, in the field, or in a virtual environment, you have to build relationships at work. When situations get challenging for you, your relationships will provide you the aircover you need to correct a mistake or get your confidence back. Relationships in the workplace are more than the friends that you eat lunch with; they are the smiles you give to others and the small conversations you make with a cubemate. They are your mentors and they are your cheerleaders.

The workplace is not a social media playground, even though some people may try and pretend it is. You should not be preoccupied by receiving "likes" for the things you say. It is true in the world as it is in the workplace that you cannot please everybody. The workplace is a forum to showcase your talents, and you cannot take criticism or someone's bad attitude toward you personally.

What people do or say should not be taken as a personal reflection of who you are. As professionals, we are more than the projects we engage in and we are more than a bad report. Like a social media playground, there will be "haters" in the workplace who try to get you to react to their bad behaviors or nasty words. Don't react. Remember the strategies you have learned about framing, self-control and self-awareness. Remember that you control your image and find comfort and strength in the relationships you've built.

Finally, turf wars and hardball politics are real among professionals and when a person, team or group feels threatened, battles can ensue. Unlike what you see on television (the obvious storylines and strict character behaviour), people can be unpredictable and, in the spirit of self-interest, they can find ways to start a conflict. Sometimes you can avoid conflicts, but, oftentimes, you find yourself in conflict and you have a choice to make. You must choose your battles wisely. In fact, the higher up the corporate ladder or rank you are, the more mindful you should be.

Whether you're just starting out in your career, or starting a new job at a new company, use the strategies in this book to gain an advantage. If you are struggling in the role you have now, or want to know how you can "lean in" more at work, use the strategies in this book to level up your career. How to succeed in the workplace tomorrow is largely based on how well you work in it today, and the best way to do that is to not just work harder, but to perform smarter.

ABOUT THE AUTHOR

Phoebe Bryant has worked in the information technology field for more than twenty years. She's a trailblazer who has held roles with increasing levels of responsibility, and now operates with executive status enveloping a solid foundation of leadership and collaboration. Her strengths in communication makes her a strong negotiator, polished diplomat, and loyal adviser to companies and entrepreneurs. Having grown up in Arizona, Phoebe is a southwest native, though she's built her entire career in the northeastern United States, where she lives today.